The Fact-Packed ACTIVITY Book
SPACE

Contents

Project Editor Radhika Haswani
Senior Editor Roohi Sehgal
Senior US Editor Shannon Beatty
US Editor Jane Perlmutter
Art Editors Bettina Myklebust Stovne, Simran Lakhiani, Bhagyashree Nayak, Mohd Zishan
Senior Art Editor Roohi Rais
Special Sales and Custom Publishing Executive Issy Walsh
Jacket Designer Rashika Kachroo
DTP Designers Sachin Gupta, Syed Md Farhan
Assistant Picture Researcher Mamta Panwar
Production Editor Dragana Puvacic
Production Controller Isabell Schart
Managing Editors Jonathan Melmoth, Monica Saigal
Managing Art Editors Diane Peyton Jones, Ivy Sengupta
Delhi Creative Heads Glenda Fernandes, Malavika Talukder
Publisher Francesca Young
Deputy Art Director Mabel Chan
Publishing Director Sarah Larter

Consultant Professor David W. Hughes

Material in this publication was previously published in:
Ultimate Factivity Collection Space (2016)

First American Edition, 2022
Published in the United States by DK Publishing
1745 Broadway, 20th Floor, New York, NY 10019

Copyright © 2022 Dorling Kindersley Limited
DK, a Division of Penguin Random House LLC
23 24 25 26 10 9 8 7 6 5 4 3 2
004-323314-Nov/2022

The rights under the copyright reserved above, no part of this publication may be reproduced, stored in or introduced into a retrieval system, or transmitted, in any form, or by any means (electronic, mechanical, photocopying, recording, or otherwise), without the prior written permission of the copyright owner.

Published in Great Britain by Dorling Kindersley Limited

A catalog record for this book is available from the Library of Congress.
ISBN 978-0-7440-5991-5

DK books are available at special discounts when purchased in bulk for sales promotions, premiums, fund-raising, or educational use. For details, contact: DK Publishing Special Markets, 1745 Broadway, 20th Floor, New York, NY 10019
SpecialSales@dk.com

Printed and bound in China

For the curious
www.dk.com

This book was made with Forest Stewardship Council™ certified paper—one small step in DK's commitment to a sustainable future. For more information go to www.dk.com/our-green-pledge

04–05	How this book works
06–07	What is space?
08–09	Where does space begin?
10–11	What's in the night sky?
12–13	Our place in space
14–15	The sun
16–17	The perfect planet
18–19	I can see the moon
20–21	Eye on the sky
22–23	Probing space
24–25	The solar system
26–27	Orbit quiz
28–29	Our solar system
30–31	Postcards from Mars
32–33	Gas giant Jupiter
34–35	Saturn's rings
36–37	Moons with a view
38–39	Shooting stars
40–41	On the surface

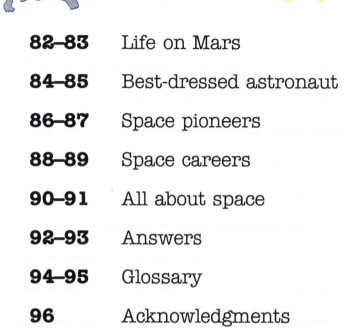

42–43	Outer space
44–45	Universe facts
46–47	Gorgeous galaxies
48–49	Star struck
50–51	Stars in the sky
52–53	A star is born
54–55	Voyage to a black hole
56–57	Amazing space!
58–59	Alien life
60–61	Going into space
62–63	Launch stages
64–65	Rockets
66–67	Space walk
68–69	The International Space Station
70–71	Other space stations
72–73	Living in space
74–75	Animals in space
76–77	Day on the moon
78–79	Rovers
80–81	Mission badges
82–83	Life on Mars
84–85	Best-dressed astronaut
86–87	Space pioneers
88–89	Space careers
90–91	All about space
92–93	Answers
94–95	Glossary
96	Acknowledgments

How this book works

Here is some information to help you find your way around this book, which is all about stars, galaxies, planets, and much more.

These boxes give you fun facts about topics.

Activities
There are many exciting activities for you to do in this book. All you need are a pen or pencil, crayons, a little imagination, and a thirst for knowledge!

Look for this roundel on every spread. It tells you what the activity is.

MATCH the moons to their descriptions. Answers on pp. 92–93.

Answers
The answers to the questions are on pp. 92–93. Good luck!

Instructions
All the instructions you'll need to complete an activity can be found on each page.

Play and Learn **Read and Learn** **Read and Create** **Draw and Learn** **Match and Learn** **Look and Find** **Test Your Knowledge**

These are the different types of activity that you will find in the book:

1 **Play and Learn:** Follow the lines or connect the dots to discover more about space and its mysteries.

2 **Read and Learn:** Read the information on the pages to learn more.

3 **Read and Create:** After reading the pages, use your coloring pens or pencils to color the pictures.

4 **Draw and Learn:** Get ready with your pencils to draw, learn, and have fun.

5 **Match and Learn:** Match the descriptions to the pictures.

6 **Look and Find:** Let's see how well you can spot the pictures in the book.

7 **Test Your Knowledge:** Test yourself by answering mind-boggling questions.

Introductions give you an overview of the topic that is being discussed on the pages.

Amazing activities will help you understand a specific topic better.

5

What is space?

Far beyond our small world is an endless stretch of cold, soundless, near-emptiness that we call space. It contains gas, dust, planets, stars, and galaxies.

FIND

where these pictures are on pp. 8–23. Check your answers on pp. 92–93.

Look and Find

Where does space begin?

Space starts at about 60 miles (100 km) above Earth's surface, where the atmosphere (the gassy shell around Earth) begins to thin before disappearing to nearly nothing. There are five layers in the atmosphere.

Extends to about 6,000 miles (10,000 km)

50–375 miles (80–600 km)

30–50 miles (50–80 km)

10–30 miles (16–50 km)

10 miles (16 km)

If you could drive to space it would take about 1 hour at 50 mph (80 kph).

Aurora Borealis (or Northern Lights)

NASA considers anyone reaching this height an astronaut.

The skydive record is 135,890 ft (41,420 m).

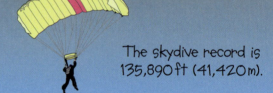
Weather balloon

Everest is the highest mountain at 29,032 ft (8,849 m).

Spy planes fly above the clouds to keep out of sight.

Cumulus clouds

Airplanes fly in the troposphere.

Look and Find

5 Up in the **exosphere** the air molecules can escape Earth's gravity and float off into space. Most satellites and space telescopes orbit here.

The Hubble Space Telescope was sent into space in 1990 to take photos of stars and planets.

COUNT the things you can spot from the list on the bottom right.

International Space Station (ISS)

4 When you reach the **thermosphere** the air is very thin. The ISS orbits in this layer, as did the first passenger space flights.

Meteors

3 Meteors burn up when they enter the **mesosphere**. The top of this layer is the coldest place on the planet.

2 The **stratosphere** contains a gas called ozone, which protects us from the sun's harmful rays. Only special jet planes can fly this high.

Cirrus clouds

1 The closest layer to the ground is the **troposphere**. It is where most of our weather happens and is the highest level at which ordinary airplanes can fly.

Which of these things can you see on these pages? Answers on pp. 92–93.

1. Skydiver
2. Meteors
3. Hot-air balloon
4. Sun
5. Clouds
6. Moon
7. Hubble Space Telescope
8. Space station

what's in the night sky?

When it gets dark, you can look up and see tiny points of light. If you have powerful binoculars, you can take a closer look at what's out there.

MATCH the descriptions to the pictures. See answers on pp. 92–93.

TRUE OR FALSE? EVERY STAR THAT YOU CAN SEE IN THE NIGHT SKY IS MORE LUMINOUS THAN THE SUN.

2 **Galaxies** are gigantic spirals of dust and gas that contain billions of stars. Our galaxy's nearest neighbor is the Andromeda galaxy.

4 **Comets** are balls of snow and rock with long, dusty tails that streak across the sky on their journey around the solar system.

3 **Constellations** are groups of stars picked out by people, which look like patterns that represent objects or animals. This is the Great Bear.

1 **Jupiter** is the largest planet in our solar system. It has swirling bands of gas and lots of moons.

We can see the features on the moon more clearly than those on Jupiter and Mars because the moon is closer to us.

10

Match and Learn

6 Mars looks like a twinkling red star. This is due to the amount of iron in its rocks. It has the tallest volcano and the longest valley of any planet we know.

Shining brightly

The brightest objects in the night sky are the moon and the planets Mercury, Venus, Mars, Jupiter, and Saturn. A visiting comet may also put on a show if it has a spectacular tail.

5 The moon is Earth's closest companion. Its surface is pitted with craters where it has been hit by meteorites.

11

Our place in space

Earth may seem big to us, but compared with the rest of space, it's incredibly tiny. So how do we fit into the scale of the unviverse?

Our star, the sun, is one of billions in our home galaxy, the **Milky Way**. We are 30,000 light-years from its center.

Earth is part of our **solar system**. It took the Voyager 2 probe 12 years to reach the solar system's farthest planet, Neptune.

The closest celestial body to **Earth** is our moon. It takes three days to get there in a crewed spacecraft.

DRAW a picture for your postcard from Al the alien.

You are here—or near somewhere like it. Even the largest cities are tiny specks when seen from space.

Light-years away

Distances in space are so enormous we measure them in light-years. Light is the fastest thing in the universe, and light-years measure how far it travels in a year—nearly 6 trillion miles (9.5 trillion km).

Draw and Learn

The Milky Way is part of the **Local Group** of galaxies. The closest of them is 200,000 light-years away.

The universe is extremely vast. It is at least 93 million light-years across and continues to expand.

I'll send you a postcard, but you need to fill in your address.

Al travels all over the universe. What has he stopped to see?

10

Name
City
Country
Planet
Star system
Galaxy
The universe

Wish you were here!
Love, Al xx

13

The sun

Stars are mostly made of **two gases**. The sun is 75% hydrogen and 24% helium, which it burns, producing light and energy.

Prominences are huge loops of gas that stretch hundreds of thousands of miles into space.

The surface of the sun is **9,900° F** (5,500° C), but its core reaches more than **27 million° F** (15 million° C).

You can fit 110 Earths across the diameter of the sun.

Solar flares are bursts of energy that show up as bright spots just above the surface.

It takes **8.2 minutes** for light to travel from the sun to Earth.

Why should we never look directly at the sun, even with sunglasses?

Because the sun is so bright its rays can burn our eyes.

14

TRUE OR FALSE?
SPACE PROBES DO NOT WARN US OF DANGEROUS SOLAR STORMS.

The sun is **4.5 billion years** old. It is about halfway through its life.

At the center of our solar system is **the sun**. The sun is a star, which astronomers call Sol. It is not a big star compared to others in the galaxy, but you could still squash 1.3 million Earths inside it.

It would take a jet airplane 20 years flying nonstop to travel the **93 million miles** (150 million km) between the sun and Earth.

Sunspots are cooler areas that appear as dark patches on the sun's face.

Storms on the sun's surface blast streams of particles into space. When the particles hit Earth's atmosphere they cause streams of light called **auroras**.

READ about the sun and discover some incredible facts related to it.

Facts about...

Future sun
In about 5 billion years the sun will **swell** and become a red giant star. It will then collapse to form an Earth-sized **white dwarf star**.

Probes keep track of the sun's activity and warn us of any dangerous solar storms heading our way.

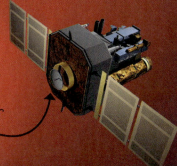

Read and Learn

15

The perfect planet

Earth is a very special place. Nowhere else in the solar system has exactly the right mix of ingredients and temperature that allow life to flourish. So what's the recipe for our perfect planet?

Oxygen: There is plenty of oxygen in the atmosphere for humans and other living things to breathe.

Water: Liquid water is vital for every form of life. It also regulates the climate.

Friendly moon: Our moon helps keep Earth rotating at a steady rate and pulls the oceans to create tides.

COLOR each ingredient and then draw an intelligent being!

Facts about...

Other Earths
Scientists searching for planets outside our solar system have found more than 4,000. Of these, **only about 800 are Earth-sized** and the right distance from their star.

Home rock
Earth is a small, rocky planet with a hot, active core. Most of its surface is covered in water. Above, is a thick, shielding atmosphere. Add in gravity to hold everything together and you have an ideal planet.

Draw and Learn

The sun: We are just the right distance from our star: too close and we would burn, too far and we would freeze.

Atmosphere: This acts as a protective blanket, keeping out harmful rays and space rocks, trapping heat, and creating weather.

Hot core: Heat from the core keeps water liquid and brings new rocks to the surface through volcanoes.

Plants: These filter out deadly carbon dioxide, make oxygen, and are a source of food for other living things.

Draw an intelligent being here. Who do you think that could be?

Nice planet, but those humans are funny-looking creatures!

Intelligent life: Earth is packed with humans and animals that have learned how to survive in all sorts of tough conditions.

17

GUESS if the statements are true or false. Answers on pp. 92-93.

The moon is Earth's companion, and it is locked to Earth so that one face points toward us and the other always points away. Different parts of the face are illuminated at different times of the month.

I can see the moon

The moon doesn't shine by itself—it reflects light from the sun.

1. The moon is **drifting away** from Earth by a distance of nearly 1.5in (4cm) every year.

2. The moon was formed when another **small planet collided** with Earth billions of years ago.

3. **Rocks** on Earth are older than those on the moon.

4. Scientists have discovered that the moon has **moonquakes** that are similar to earthquakes here on Earth.

5. The **dwarf planet Pluto** is smaller than the moon.

6. The moon isn't spherical—it's slightly **lemon shaped**, with one of the pointed ends facing Earth.

From Earth, you can see at least 30,000 craters on the visible side of the moon.

I wonder if it's really made of green cheese? I'd like a snack!

18

Southern Hemisphere

People south of the equator see the moon's phases start on the left-hand edge and move across to light up the right-hand edge.

Test Your Knowledge

Color in the changing face of the moon: yellow (y) for the sunlit area and black (b) for the unlit part.

Changing moon

We always see the same face of the moon, but how much of it is lit up depends on its position between us and the sun. From an invisible new moon it slowly grows (waxes) until the whole surface is lit. It then shrinks (wanes) until it is dark again.

New Moon — The moon is between Earth and the sun, so it looks black to us.

Waxing Crescent

Waning Crescent

First Quarter

Last Quarter

Turn the page to see the view from below the equator

On the equator

From here you see the waxing crescent start at the top edge of the moon. The waning crescent appears at the bottom.

Waxing Gibbous

Waning Gibbous

Full Moon — At a full moon, all of the moon's face is lit by sunlight.

Earth

Turn the page to see the view from the equator

Northern Hemisphere

If you live north of the equator, the moon starts to light up from the right-hand edge and finishes on the left-hand edge.

Eye on the Sky

X-rays reveal the hidden structure of galaxies, such as the Cartwheel galaxy, as seen by the Chandra X-ray Observatory.

Space optical telescopes, such as Hubble, can see galaxies like the Antennae better than those on Earth.

FOLLOW the lines to match each picture to the correct telescope.

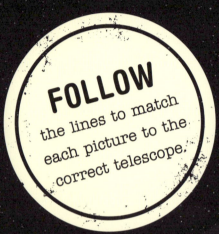

Space telescopes
Putting a telescope in space lets astronomers detect light that can't get through Earth's atmosphere.

Microwaves and **infrared** are used to look for hot objects hidden by dust, such as this star nursery.

Radio astronomy searches for energy sources, such as pulsars and matter falling into black holes.

We use telescopes to see distant objects in the sky more clearly. These tools collect different kinds of light and turn it into images that we would otherwise not be able to see. The larger the telescope, the greater the detail we can see.

Ground telescopes
Land-based observatories use optical, radio, or microwave telescopes. They are usually built in remote, dry places high above the clouds.

Match and Learn

Gamma rays are emitted by high-energy objects, such as the black hole in the galaxy Centaurus A.

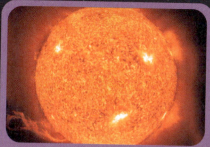

Ultraviolet light is used by solar observatories, such as SOHO, to watch the activity of the sun.

The telescope Spitzer's **infrared** detectors pick up the heat from dying stars, such as the Helix nebula.

Optical telescopes collect visible light using mirrors and lenses. This cluster is called the Jewel Box.

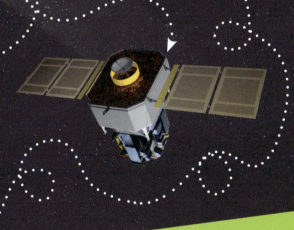

Facts about...

First light

Telescopes have enabled us to see some of the **oldest stars and galaxies** in the universe. One such star is **13.6 billion years old** and is still shining—but only just.

Probing space

Most of what we know about our solar system has come from sending out probes. These uncrewed spacecraft analyze, photograph, and send data back to Earth. Some just fly past their target, while others go into orbit or send smaller probes down to the surface.

TRACE the path of each probe to the right planet.

Liftoff from Earth

1
2
3
4
5

Messenger is the only probe to have orbited **Mercury** and mapped its surface.

New Horizons took the first ever close-up pictures of **Pluto** in July 2015.

Voyager 2 flew past **Neptune** in 1989. It has not been visited since then.

Nine spacecraft have visited **Jupiter**. They are *Pioneer 10, Pioneer 11, Voyager 1, Voyager 2, Ulysses, Cassini, New Horizons, Galileo,* and *Juno*.

The *Cassini* spacecraft burned out in the **Saturnian** atmosphere on September 15, 2017.

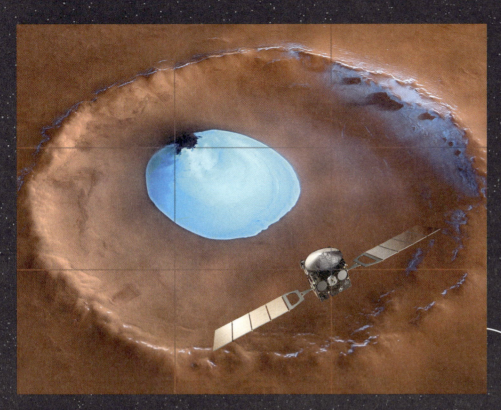

Ice spy...

This huge sheet of water ice was spotted in a Martian crater by the Mars Express probe. The probe's mission is to map the surface of Mars and analyze its rocks and atmosphere.

Draw and Learn

Copy the picture of the Mars Express flying over the crater, and color it in.

23

The solar system

Earth is one of eight planets that go around our sun. Moons, dwarf planets, asteroids, and the occasional visiting comet are also members of the solar system family.

Orbit quiz

The planets go around the sun in a regular path called an orbit. It takes Earth a year to make one trip. Planets closer to the sun take less time, while those farther out take much longer.

1 **Mercury** is the smallest and fastest-orbiting planet.

2 **Venus** is Earth's hotter and faster twin planet.

3 **Earth** is the fifth-largest planet in the solar system.

4 **Mars** takes twice as long to orbit as Earth.

Facts about... The Kuiper Belt

This is a **ring of icy and frozen objects** that lies just beyond Neptune. It largely contains rocks, comets, and a few dwarf planets.

26

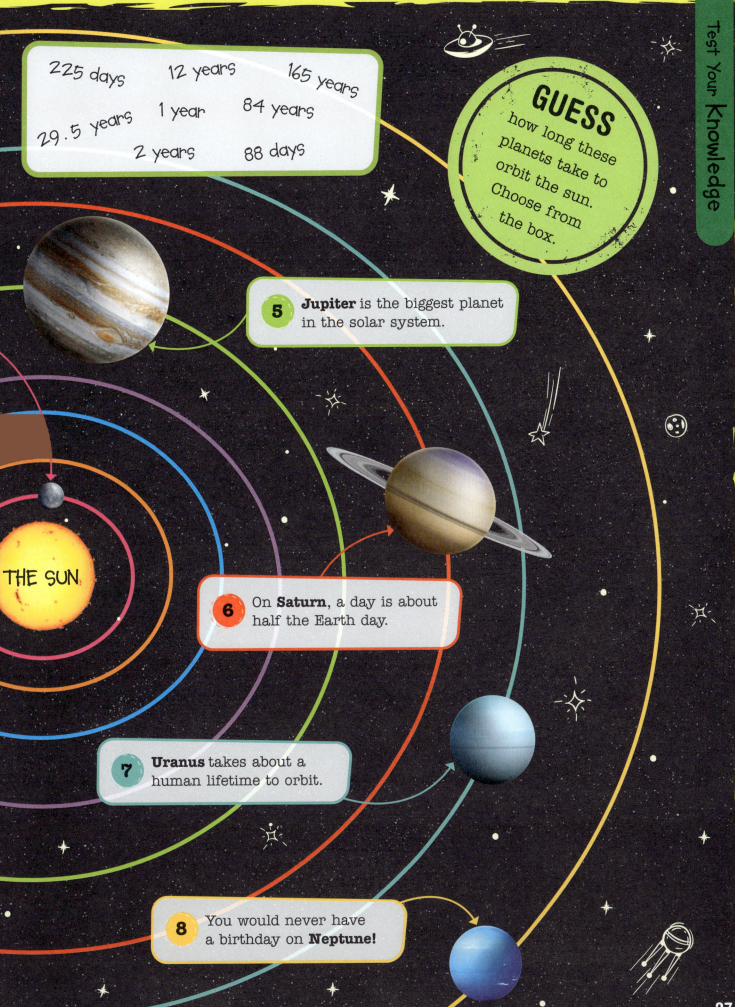

The **sun** is the source of light and heat for all the planets in our solar system. The farther you are from it, the colder and darker it gets.

Near and far
There is an enormous difference between the inner and outer planets. Those closest to the sun are small and rocky, while those farther out are freezing-cold gas giants.

MATCH the celestial objects to their descriptions. See answers on pp. 92–93.

Hello! This is where we live.

Saturn is the second-largest planet, but its particles are so loosely packed it would float in water.

Neptune is an ice giant and farthest from the sun. The winds here are the fastest in the solar system.

Mars is small and cold. It may once have had liquid water, but now it is a dry, rusty-red desert.

Uranus spins on its side after being knocked over early in its life. Its rings and moons rotate up and over the planet.

Facts about...

The asteroid belt
Scientists believe that asteroids are fragments that were left over after the formation of the solar system. There are **billions of them**, but most are less than 0.6 miles (1 km) wide. They are usually named after people, but some have more unusual names such as Dizzy, Dodo, Brontosaurus, Wombat, and Humptydumpty.

28

Our solar system

A group of planets orbiting a star is called a planetary system. This also includes the moons of the planets, asteroids, comets, and smaller pieces of rock and dust. Our planetary system is called the solar system.

Match and Learn

The **asteroid belt** is a wide band of rocky debris that lies between Mars and Jupiter.

This planet's rings are mostly ice and dust, probably from a smashed moon.

Earth is the largest of the four inner planets. It is the only place in the solar system where life is known to exist.

Venus is similar in size to Earth, but it is incredibly hot and is cloaked in thick yellow clouds that rain acid.

Mercury is the smallest planet. Its surface is covered with craters, so it looks similiar to our moon.

7

Jupiter is the largest planet. The stripes on its face are bands of clouds that swirl into giant storms like the Great Red Spot.

8

The rings are made of dark dust and rocky material.

9

29

Postcards from Mars

Other than Earth, Mars is the most explored planet in the solar system. Four robotic rovers have crawled over its surface, and over 40 probes have orbited around it. This is a tour of the must-see sights on Mars.

COLOR the rovers on these pages.

Olympus Mons

This is the largest volcano in the solar system. It's three times the height of Mount Everest and almost as wide as France. Wow!

Hi, I'm Curiosity, a rover on Mars, and your guide for this tour. Let's go and explore! First stop, Olympus Mons.

Sand dunes
Mars is as dry as a desert and covered in sand. The wind blows the sand into huge, crescent-shaped dunes. These are made of dark volcanic sand.

Dust devil tracks
Sometimes the winds create mini tornadoes called dust devils. These lift the lighter sand off the surface to reveal the darker sand beneath it. Pretty, isn't it?

Santa Maria crater

This stadium-sized crater was formed by a large meteor impact. It's young compared with some craters around here, but is old enough to have formed some sand dunes in the middle of it.

Wow—I never knew there was so much to see here!

Valles Marineris

Five times deeper and 10 times longer than the US's Grand Canyon, this valley system stretches a fifth of the way around Mars. It's a long way to the bottom!

Martian blueberries

These pebbly spheres are full of iron. On Earth, mineral balls like these form in lakes, so they may be proof that there was once water on Mars.

North Pole

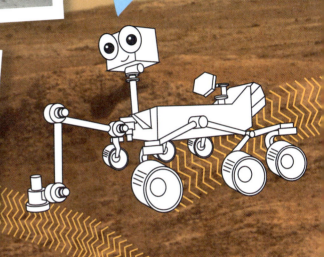

The ice here is about 620 miles (1,000 km) across and 1.2 miles (2 km) thick. It's mostly ice water, but in winter it's so cold that carbon dioxide gas freezes and falls as snow.

Sunset

At the end of the day there's nothing better than watching the sun go down. Sunsets are blue on Mars because of the way that red dust in the atmosphere scatters light. Time to shut down the batteries!

Play and Learn

31

Gas giant Jupiter

Jupiter is truly the king of the planets. This giant ball of gas has two-and-a-half times more mass than all the other planets put together.

ANSWER the questions given in the quiz box. See answers on pp. 92–93.

This is how big Earth is compared to Jupiter.

Inside the giant
Jupiter doesn't have a solid surface. Its atmosphere is 3,100 miles (5,000 km) deep. Beneath it are layers of liquid and metallic hydrogen and helium. There may just be a small, hot, rocky core, however, at the center.

Jupiter's stripes are bands of clouds that race around the planet at slightly different speeds.

White ovals are small storms in the cold upper atmosphere.

Many moons

Ganymede

Callisto

Io

Europa

Jupiter has 79 known moons. The four largest moons are Ganymede, Callisto, Io, and Europa. The first three are bigger than our moon, and Ganymede is also bigger than the planet Mercury.

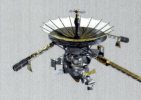

Galileo was the first spacecraft to orbit Jupiter and investigate its weather and moons.

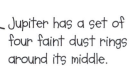

Jupiter has a set of four faint dust rings around its middle.

A great spot for storms

Storms on Jupiter can last for ages. The Great Red Spot is a high-pressure region where a storm has been raging for at least 400 years. It is roughly the width of Earth, but is slowly shrinking.

Facts about...

In a spin

Jupiter rotates faster than any of the other planets. A day there only lasts **10 hours**. It spins so fast, the speed makes its equator bulge outward.

Quiz

1. What is Jupiter's atmosphere made of?
2. How many moons does Jupiter have?
3. What was the Galileo mission?
4. How long is a day on Jupiter?

Test Your Knowledge

Saturn's rings

Saturn is possibly the most beautiful of all the planets. It is surrounded by an icy ring system that is so large and bright that it shines when seen through a telescope.

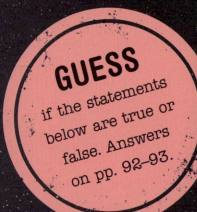

GUESS if the statements below are true or false. Answers on pp. 92–93.

Ring king
Saturn's rings are 175,000 miles (280,000 km) wide but are usually less than 0.6 miles (1 km) thick. There are three main and six minor rings, and a few incomplete arcs.

Stunning Saturn quiz

1 **Saturn** is the only planet that would float in water—if you could find a bathtub big enough to put it in.

2 The temperature at Saturn's **south pole** is much hotter than that at its equator.

3 The rings of Saturn were **first seen in 1969** by the first man on the moon, Neil Armstrong.

4 Saturn is the **most distant planet** that can be seen without the aid of a telescope.

34

← Saturn's polar regions look blue in winter.

← Its bands of cloud are not as clear as those on Jupiter, but the weather is just as stormy.

I've been going around this ring for days. Where's the exit?

Facts about...

Inner moons
Some of Saturn's moons orbit inside gaps in its rings. Called **shepherd moons**, these keep the edges of the rings tidy by herding stray lumps of ice back into it.

Test Your Knowledge

Icy halo
Unlike the dust rings of the other gas giants, Saturn's rings are covered with ice. The pieces vary in size from tiny crystals to icebergs as big as a house. They are constantly clumping together and smashing apart.

5 Saturn is **three times** farther away from the sun than Jupiter.

35

Moons with a view

The outer planets of our solar system have a lot of moons, while the inner planets have very few moons or none at all. Moons are made of rock and ice, and offer some of the most spectacular scenery in the solar system.

MATCH the pictures to their descriptions. Answers on pp. 92–93.

How many moons?

There are more than 200 moons orbiting the planets. Here, we list how many moons each planet has.

Mercury	Venus	Earth
0	0	1

4

 Our own **moon** is a gray, airless world. Its outer crust was once molten lava but is now covered in craters made by meteorites hitting the surface after it cooled.

 Titan is Saturn's largest moon. Huge lakes of liquid methane lie near its poles—two fixed points at the opposite ends of a planet. The atmosphere is thick and smoggy, and its brown clouds rain methane.

5

 Ganymede is the biggest moon in the solar system. A chain of craters across its surface show where the fragments of a comet pulled by Jupiter's gravity slammed into it.

 On Uranus's moon, **Miranda**, is a long cliff that is six times higher than the Grand Canyon. A rock dropped from the top would take 10 minutes to hit the bottom because of the moon's low gravity.

6

 Enceladus is a tiny, icy moon of Saturn. Beneath its snowy crust is warm water that gets blasted upward as jets made of icy crystals.

 Volcanically active **Triton** is Neptune's largest moon. Its huge eruptions of nitrogen gas and dust can last a whole year.

Match and Learn

Mars	Jupiter	Saturn	Uranus	Neptune
2	79	82	27	14

This is such interesting information!

Shooting stars

Different space rocks

If you look up on a clear night you may see a sudden streak of light flash across the sky. This is almost certainly a shooting star, or meteor, which is a fiery space rock.

Meteoroids are lumps of space rock. Most are fragments left behind by comets and are the size of a grain of sand, but some are really huge.

When meteoroids enter Earth's atmosphere they become **meteors**. They travel so fast through the atmosphere that they light up as shooting stars.

GUESS if the statements are true or false. Answers on pp. 92–93.

A **meteorite** is a meteoroid that has survived its journey through the atmosphere and has landed on Earth. Most meteorites fall into the ocean.

Most meteors come from the surface of Mars or the moon.

Asteroids sometimes fall to Earth in huge fireballs. The results can be disastrous—one is thought to have caused the extinction of the dinosaurs.

Around 48.5 tons (44 tonnes) of meteorites land on Earth every day.

Meteor showers occur quite often throughout the year. The Leonids is a shower that appears in November and comes from a known comet, Tempel-Tuttle. Hundreds of meteors an hour can be seen.

Fewer than 100 meteorites have ever been found.

Meteor showers only happen once a year.

Some meteors are bigger than a house.

The International Space Station is regularly mistaken for a meteor.

The moon has a lot of craters because it has no atmosphere to burn up meteoroids.

Oooh look—a shooting star!

Facts about... Impact craters

Meteorites that hit land form **bowl-shaped craters**. Earth has been hit many times, but most craters have worn away. Some, however, like **Meteor Crater** in the US, are still visible.

39

On the surface

All the planets and moons in our solar system look very different. Some are bare rock, some have atmospheres, others are balls of gas, while many of the worlds farthest out are locked in ice.

Jupiter: This planet has a thick atmosphere of gases that churn and swirl at very fast speeds to create different colored bands. Large spots show areas where storms are raging.

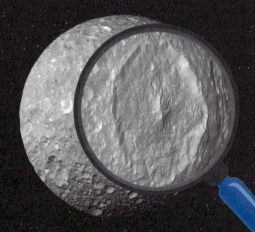

Mimas: This moon of Saturn is mostly ice with a small amount of rock. Its surface is covered in craters. The largest crater, Herschel, is the result of an impact that nearly shattered the moon completely.

Io: The face of this moon of Jupiter looks like a pizza because of volcanoes that are constantly erupting lava onto its surface. The lava contains a lot of sulfur, which gives Io its yellow, orange, and black colors.

Pluto: This dwarf planet was shown to have a big heart-shaped, nitrogen-ice filled crater. Pluto is reddish in color and has many mountains and craters on its surface.

Pluto's "heart"

Europa: Jupiter's fourth-largest moon has an icy surface that is crisscrossed with lines. These cracks are probably caused by tidal movement. The thick ice crust is above a deep, salty, liquid-water ocean.

DRAW and color in the surface of your own planet.

Earth: Our planet is unique in the solar system since most of its surface is covered in water. This makes it look blue from space, with greenish-brown areas of land, and wispy white clouds in the atmosphere.

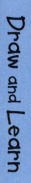

Draw and Learn

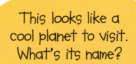

This looks like a cool planet to visit. What's its name?

41

Outer space

Our universe is almost too huge to imagine, packed with billions of galaxies and trillions of stars and planets. It is so big, we are only able to see a small part of it.

Universe facts

There are so many fascinating facts to learn about the unviverse. Take this quiz and see how much you know already!

1 The unviverse was formed in an explosion called the Big Bang around **13.7 billion years ago**.

GUESS if these eight statements are true or false. Answers on pp. 92–93.

2 The unviverse is **constantly expanding**—but it has no center or edges.

3 Astronomers estimate that around **275 stars are born or die** in the unviverse every day.

"We read so much about space in school, but there is still a lot more to unravel and learn!"

Test Your Knowledge

This picture is of an area of sky barely the size of a postage stamp. It looks empty when seen with the naked eye from Earth, but when the Hubble Telescope took a closer look, it was found to contain around 10,000 galaxies.

Hubble Space Telescope

4 Jupiter is like a **cosmic sweeping brush**, scattering asteroids throughout the solar system.

5 There is a huge cloud of gas near the center of the Milky Way that **smells like cabbage**.

6 Space suits protect astronauts from **dust, debris, radiation,** and **temperature changes** in space.

7 The US launched the world's **first artificial satellite**, Sputnik 1.

8 Jupiter is so large, it can fit more than **1,000 Earths** inside it.

45

Galaxy shapes

Galaxies are collections of stars. There are three main types: spirals, ellipticals, and irregular. Most are dwarf galaxies, and many are believed to have a black hole at their center.

MATCH the description of each galaxy with its type. See answers on pp. 92–93.

We can see our own galaxy, the **Milky Way**, but we only see it as a band of stars and dust stretching across the night sky, because we are in one of the spiral arms.

Hmm, which is which? Try reading all the clues first.

- **a** Irregular
- **b** Barred spiral
- **c** Dwarf
- **d** Spiral
- **e** Elliptical

1 Spiraling like cosmic fireworks, these galaxies trail long arms of gas, dust, and stars around a bright center.

2 These fuzzy, oval-shaped galaxies contain mostly old yellow and red stars with little or no gas or dust between them.

Gorgeous galaxies

So pretty! The Milky Way is a barred spiral galaxy.

Match and Learn

3 The core of this galaxy is stretched out into a central bar of stars. Two long, trailing arms spiral out from each end of the bar.

4 Full of gas, dust, and hot blue stars, these galaxies don't have a regular shape. They may be the result of two galaxies colliding.

It's much easier to see stars when you're far away from the bright lights of towns and cities, such as at this observatory.

Galaxies are among the most spectacular sights seen through a telescope. There are at least 170 billion of them in the universe, each containing millions, billions, or even trillions of stars.

5 These smaller galaxies can be spiral, elliptical, or irregular in shape, but are only around one-hundredth the size of the Milky Way.

Starstruck

There are more stars in the unviverse than we can imagine. They're not, however, all the same—there are different types that vary in size and temperature. Some are close to blowing up!

Red dwarf

Example: Proxima Centauri
Life story: These are the most common stars in the unviverse. They are cooler and much less massive than our sun, and very dim, but may burn for trillions of years.

Main sequence star

Example: The sun
Life story: Average stars like our sun are called main sequence stars. Depending on their mass, they eventually turn into blue or red giants, or into dwarfs.

Born in the clouds

Stars form in vast clouds of gas and dust. As they grow larger they eventually ignite, blasting jets of radiation through the cloud and sculpting it into unusual shapes that glow in space.

White dwarf

Example: HD 62166 in the constellation Puppis
Life story: When a red giant runs out of hydrogen it collapses in on itself to form a hot white dwarf. It slowly cools down to become a solid, cold, black dwarf.

Supernova

Example: SN 1987A in the constellation Dorado
Life story: A supernova is a giant star that has become unstable and has exploded. It is seen as a sudden burst of light as it flings its atoms into space.

LEARN about different types of stars and their qualities.

Red giant

Example: Betelgeuse in the constellation Orion

Life story: Once a main sequence star has used up all its hydrogen gas, it starts to burn helium. The star expands, but because its outer layer is cooler, it looks red.

Blue giant

Example: Alcyone in Taurus's star cluster the Pleiades

Life story: Blue giants are smaller and much hotter than red giants. They are very bright, but quickly run out of fuel and turn into a supernova.

Neutron star

Typical star: Crab pulsar in the constellation Taurus

Life story: Neutron stars are tiny but incredibly hot and heavy. Some rotate hundreds of times a second. Pulsars are neutron stars that emit radiation as they spin.

Read and Learn

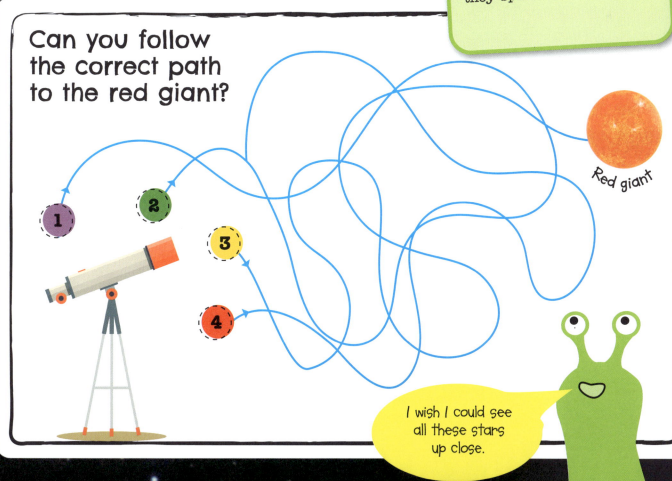

Can you follow the correct path to the red giant?

I wish I could see all these stars up close.

49

Stars in the sky

For millennia, people have been spotting patterns of stars that we call constellations. The constellations are mostly animals, objects, or figures from mythology.

CONNECT the dots to reveal one of the best-known constellations.

Cassiopeia was a mythical queen. The five main stars form a sideways W. The central star in the W points to the northern polestar.

Leo, the Lion, is easily recognizable from the sickle shape of its head and chest. It is one of a group of 12 constellations called the zodiac.

Cygnus, the Swan, contains the bright star Deneb in its tail. This area of the sky is full of nebulas and star clusters.

Crux, the Southern Cross, is the smallest of all the constellations. The bottom star of the long arm points toward the South Pole.

Ancient shapes

There are 88 officially named constellations. More than half of them were first drawn over 2,000 years ago by observers near the Mediterranean Sea.

Night hunter

One of the best-known constellations is Orion, the Hunter. It is easy to spot because of the three close stars in his belt and the bright stars Betelgeuse and Rigel.

This is what Orion looks like in the sky.

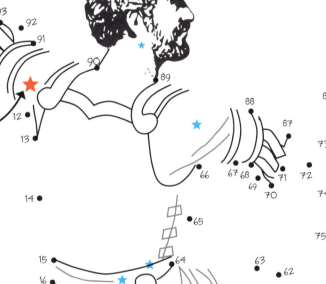

Betelgeuse is a red supergiant.

Orion is shown carrying a club and either a shield, a bow and arrows, or the head of a lion.

The Orion Nebula can be seen in the sword hanging from his belt.

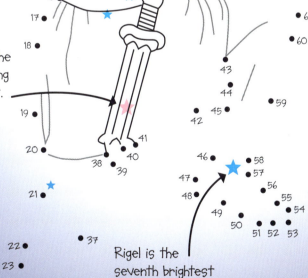

Rigel is the seventh brightest star in the sky.

Facts about... On the move

While stars may look close together, most are at different distances from us. They are also moving, so the patterns we see today are **not exactly the same** as the ancients saw them.

Draw and Learn

51

A star is born

All over the universe, stars are being born. The life cycle of a star depends on its mass, which also determines how it eventually dies.

New stars form inside gas and dust.

Hypergiants are enormous but short-lived stars. They quickly become unstable, throwing off some gas instead of burning it.

Large protostar

When **protostars** get so hot that they reach 10 million K (Kelvins), they ignite to become a star.

Blue supergiants are hot, massive stars. They burn hydrogen very quickly and last for a few million years.

Average stars like our sun burn slowly and last for billions of years.

Small protostars have less gas and make smaller stars.

TRUE OR FALSE?
MOST BLUE SUPERGIANTS END AS NEUTRON STARS.

Star nursery

Most stars begin as a cold cloud of hydrogen gas and dust, called a **nebula**. If the cloud is dense enough it starts to form swirling clumps that get tighter and hotter, creating **protostars**.

Read and Learn

Black holes form from the supernovas of really massive hypergiants. We can't see them because their gravity is so strong that light can't escape from them.

If the star is unstable enough, it may simply explode in a **supernova** without going through another stage.

If the star has enough mass it may form a small **black hole**.

READ about the life cycle of a star and what stars are made up of.

These stars expand into **red supergiants** and start to burn other elements.

When it has used up all its fuel, the star collapses, causing a huge explosion called a **supernova**.

Most blue supergiants end their days as a tiny, extremely dense, fast-spinning **neutron star**.

Watch out for the black hole!

When the star runs out of hydrogen it expands into a **red giant** and starts to burn helium.

Once its helium is gone, the star blows off its outer layers and becomes a **planetary nebula**.

What remains is a small, white-hot core. This **white dwarf** slowly cools until it loses all its heat.

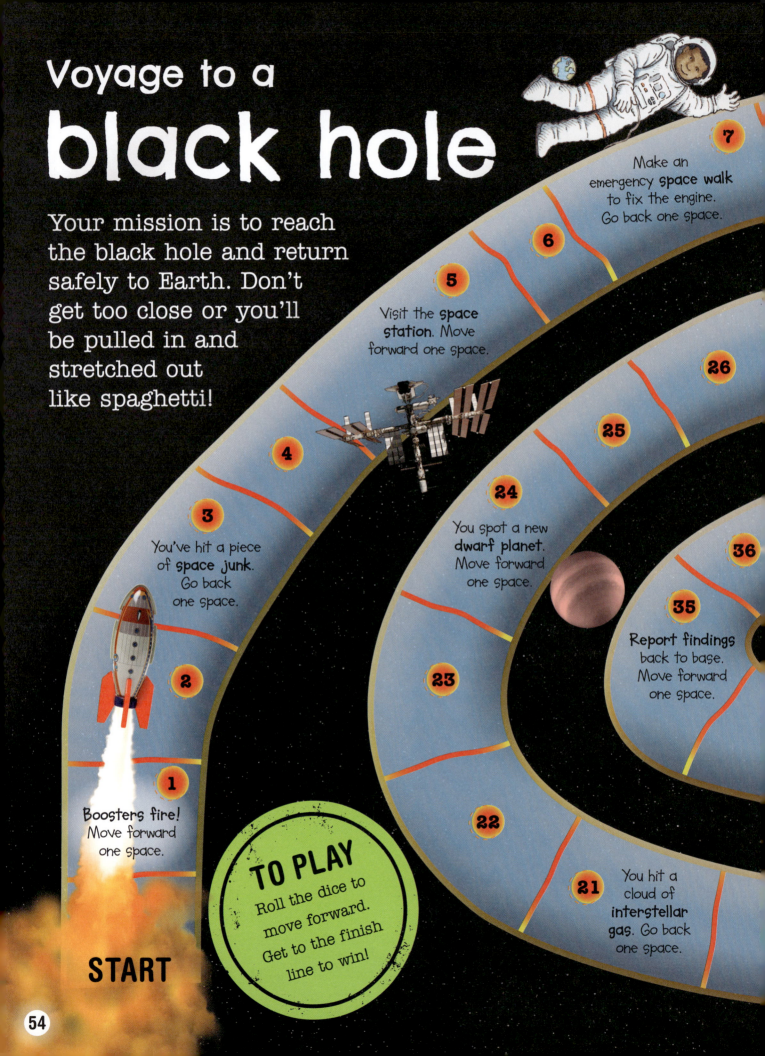

a

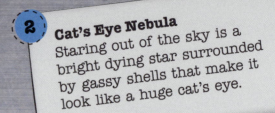

2 Cat's Eye Nebula
Staring out of the sky is a bright dying star surrounded by gassy shells that make it look like a huge cat's eye.

3 Butterfly Nebula
These delicate butterfly's wings are actually jets of oxygen and carbon-rich dust being hurled out at supersonic speeds.

b

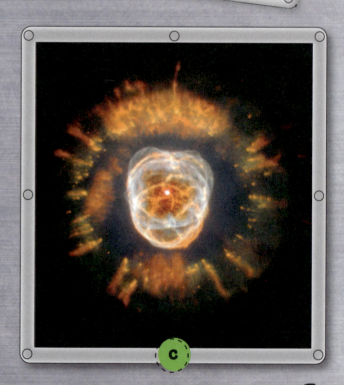

c

1 Carina Nebula
These long fingers of dust hide new stars. The hornlike spikes are jets of gas being fired out by the super-hot baby stars inside.

Amazing space!

Space is full of huge clouds of dust and gas called nebulae. Some of them are places where new stars are born. Others are the remains of dying stars that are flinging their outer layers of gas deep into space.

MATCH the nebulae to their descriptions. See answers on pp. 92–93.

Match and Learn

d

6 **Eskimo Nebula**
This nebula, made of bubbles of gas blown by a dying star and surrounded by streamers, was thought to look like a face inside a furry hood.

e

4 **Horsehead Nebula**
Like a dark horse, this tiny part of the Orion Nebula rears out of the red clouds of gas around it.

5 **Small Magellanic Cloud**
Hot, bright stars have formed in this area of our neighboring galaxy. They are blasting out radiation that lights up the gas clouds.

f

g

7 **Orion Nebula**
Hanging in Orion's sword is this huge nebula, which is creating new stars and solar systems, complete with baby planets.

57

What makes you think an alien will look like me?

Alien life

With so many planets orbiting other stars, it is likely that life exists elsewhere in the universe. We call such life aliens, and they could even look like Earth animals.

Aliens in stories are usually based on humans.

Hot planets

Planets that are close to their star are likely to be hot and dry. Life there may be similiar to our own desert animals—camels, scorpions, lizards, meerkats, and ostriches—that can survive without much water.

This thorny devil is a spiky Australian desert lizard.

The pull of gravity

Gravity affects how life can grow and move. If gravity is high, animals are likely to move slowly and be close to the ground. With low gravity, life can move more easily and grow tall.

Color in the two aliens on this page.

Sluglike animals may survive on high-gravity planets.

Opabinia is no alien— it once lived on Earth!

Watery worlds

Animals that live in water have to be able to swim or float. They may have big eyes or lights to see in the dark, fins, scaly skin, or a flabby body to deal with the pressure.

Facts about...

Space bears

Tardigrades, or water bears, are like **little aliens**, complete with their **own space suit**. They can survive living in space for up to **10 days** without harm.

Icy cold

Planets far from a star are cold and dark. Animals here may have thick coats; a good layer of fat; small feet, ears, and noses; and feelers to find their way.

Planet name: _____

1. Hot
2. Watery
3. Cold
4. Dry
5. Low gravity
6. High gravity

You can name your planet and also choose the conditions it will have. Some of them are listed here.

DRAW and color an alien that could live on the type of planet you have chosen.

Draw and Learn

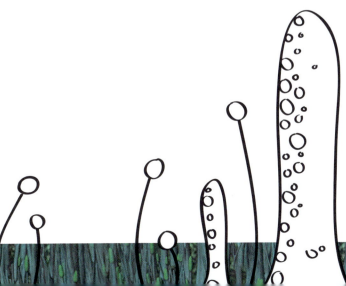

Going into space

Exploring space isn't easy. Even getting off the ground is hard! You also have to take everything you need—air, food, water, and fuel.

FIND
where these pictures are on pp. 62–91. Check your answers on pp. 92–93.

Look and Find

7

8

9

10

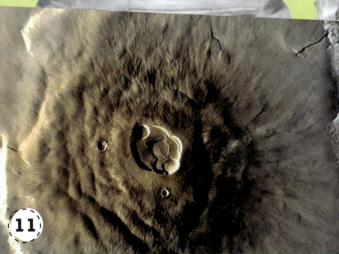
11

12

61

Launch stages

READ and learn about the different stages of a rocket launch.

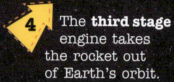

5 The **Apollo spacecraft** travels on toward the moon.

4 The **third stage** engine takes the rocket out of Earth's orbit.

3 The **second stage** burns for 6 minutes, taking the rocket to a height of 115 miles (185 km) before it falls back to Earth.

A Launch Escape rocket would eject the Command Module to safety if there is a problem during launch.

The Apollo Command and Service Module

Third stage

2 The **first stage** detaches when it has used up its fuel and the rocket is 32 miles (68 km) above the ground.

Second stage

First stage

5, 4, 3, 2, 1... It takes an enormous amount of power and speed to escape Earth's gravity and go into space. The **Saturn V** (left), which took people to the moon, is the most powerful rocket ever to be launched. It weighed as much as 400 elephants when fully fueled.

1 **Launch:** The main engines on the first stage fire, producing as much power as 543 jet fighters.

The noise at liftoff can be deadly if you're too close.

62

Help your rocket find its way to the moon!

Play and Learn

63

Rockets

If you want to go into space, you need a rocket. Nothing else has the power or speed to escape Earth's gravity. A trip aboard one of these high-flying machines takes a lot of courage.

Facts about... Rocket science

Rockets were first invented in China in the **12th century**. They were used with arrows, powered by burning gunpowder, and used as weapons.

Delta II: A smaller rocket that has been on more than 150 successful missions.

Soyuz: These Russian rockets are used to take astronauts and cargo to the International Space Station.

Space Shuttle: The shuttle couldn't launch itself, so it had to be strapped to three large rockets.

Delta IV Heavy: Currently, the only rocket capable of lifting heavy cargo into a moon or Mars orbit.

Falcon 9: A two-stage rocket that can carry satellites or deliver supplies to the International Space Station.

Saturn V: This three-stage rocket was used to launch the Apollo spacecraft on missions to the moon.

Ariane 6: This rocket is planned for a launch in 2022 to put heavy and light payloads into a wide range of orbits.

Long March 9: China will be using this rocket to send its taikonauts to the moon by 2030.

DRAW
a rocket that can take you on a trip to outer space!

Draw and Learn

New rockets are being tested for future missions to Mars.

Space walk

When astronauts travel outside the spacecraft, it is called a space walk, or Extravehicular Activity (EVA). Astronauts go on space walks to work on the spacecraft, explore, or conduct experiments. They wear space suits for safety.

SPOT five differences between the two pictures shown below.

Facts about...

First walk
On March 18, 1965, **Alexei Leonov**, a Russian cosmonaut, took the first ever space walk. He drifted in space for **12 minutes and 9 seconds.**

Look and Find

Oh wow! Space suits look so cool. I'd love to wear one!

67

The International Space Station

Astronauts have been living in space for many years aboard the International Space Station (ISS). It has been occupied for over 21 years, goes around Earth every 93 minutes, and is 250 miles (400 km) up. On average it hosts seven astronauts but this number can go up to 12.

TRUE OR FALSE?
BRUCE MCCANDLESS WAS THE FIRST ASTRONAUT TO MAKE AN UNATTACHED SPACE WALK.

Facts about...

Trusses
A **356 ft (109 m) truss** system forms the **backbone** of the station. It supports the solar panels, carries electric and communications cables, and houses spare parts and the track for the robotic arms.

The main **robot arm** is used for lifting astronauts and equipment. There is a smaller arm on the Kibo laboratory.

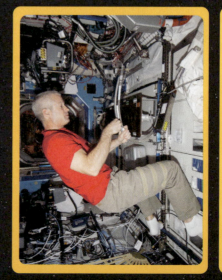

There are **three laboratories** on the ISS. Up to 150 experiments are conducted, mostly on the effects of low gravity and on the health of the astronauts.

READ about life on the International Space Station.

Read and Learn

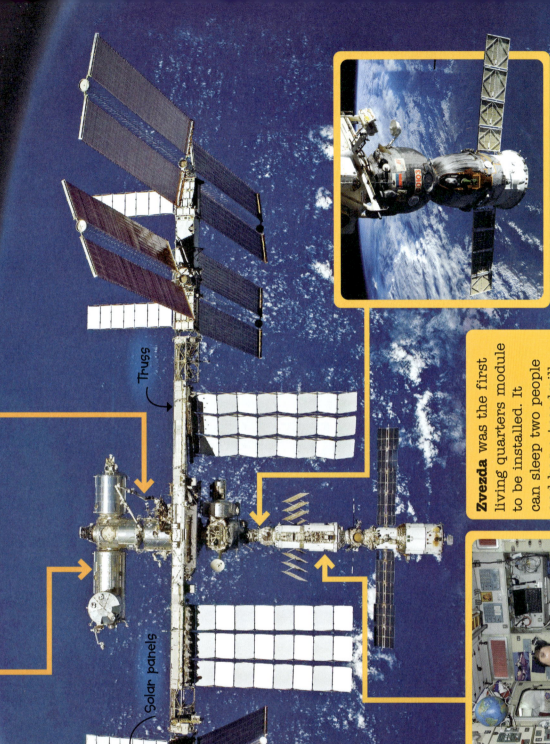

Truss

Solar panels

Docking stations enable rockets to bring new crews and supplies to the ISS every few months.

Zvezda was the first living quarters module to be installed. It can sleep two people and has a treadmill, kitchen, and toilet. It controls the ISS's life-support systems.

There are two **air locks** that allow astronauts to make space walks outside the ISS, and one to release payloads into space.

69

Other space stations

Astronauts stay on space stations and study how things work in very low gravity. We've already read about the ISS, so let's take a look at some other famous space stations, too!

Skylab (1973)
Skylab, NASA's first space station, was put together using part of a Saturn V rocket. It was used for testing how crews could manage weightlessness over a long period of time.

1 When was Skylab launched into space?

Salyut 7 (1982)
Salyut 7 was the Soviet Union's (now Russia's) final Salyut space station in the series. It stayed in orbit for about nine years and helped scientists work on technology that was later used in the development of Mir.

2 How long did Salyut 7 remain in orbit?

Test Your Knowledge

Mir (1986)

It took the Soviet Union (now Russia) 10 years to put together Mir, the world's first large space station. It was occupied by astronauts, from 12 different countries, until 2000.

FIND the answers to the questions. Check answers on pp. 92–93.

3 Which country launched the world's first large space station?

I had no idea about these space stations. There is so much to learn and see.

Tiangong 1 (2011)

Tiangong-1 was China's first space station. Chinese astronauts stayed here in 2012 and 2013 to conduct experiments. Tiangong-1 burned up while reentering Earth's atmosphere in 2018.

4 How long was Tiangong-1 in service?

The survivor
Mir survived **15 years** in orbit, which was three times its planned duration. It was home to **125 astronauts** during its lifetime.

Facts about...

71

Living in space

High above Earth, the ISS is home to a crew of astronauts. They live and work in a space that is totally crammed with equipment and gadgets.

Strap yourself in for a good night's sleep!

Washing hair needs special no-rinse soap.

Daily exercise is vital to keep bones and muscles healthy.

Grab rail

Solar panels provide power.

Daily routine

Every detail of an astronaut's day is planned years before they leave Earth. There are set times for eating, working, exercising, and maintaining the station. At the end of the day there is time to relax and call home.

COLOR the inside of the International Space Station.

Animals in space

Before people went into space, many animals including dogs, spiders, rabbits, cats, chimpanzees, and mice were sent there to see if space was safe for humans. Let's read about some of them.

Little Martha

In 1959, Little Martha became the first rabbit to go into space. Accompanied by two dogs, she went on a suborbital flight.

Laika

In 1957, Laika became the first animal to orbit Earth. She was a stray dog found on the streets of Moscow, Russia.

Play and Learn

Félicette
In 1963, Félicette became the only cat to go into space. After spending 15 minutes there, she parachuted safely to Earth.

FOLLOW
the lines to match the animal names to their correct pictures.

Arabella
In 1973, two spiders, Arabella and Anita, were sent to the Skylab space station. They were able to spin webs in zero gravity!

Ham
Ham, a four-year-old chimpanzee, was launched into space in 1961. He lived for another 22 years after his return to Earth.

Day on the moon

Only 12 people have ever set foot on the moon. It is a difficult place to stay because it has no air to breathe and no water, but we still think it's worth a visit! Come along with us.

COLOR the pictures to show what the astronauts did on the moon.

1 After a journey of 240,000 miles (385,000 km), we fire the retro rockets on the Lunar Module and land on the moon. Our pilot is orbiting above us in the Command Module.

2 We finally set foot on the surface. It's very dusty and gray, with lumps of rock and small craters everywhere. The first thing to do is plant a flag and take a few snapshots.

3 There is plenty of work to do here—collecting rock and soil samples, testing for moonquakes, and measuring the magnetic field. We film everything for the scientists back home.

4 Time for a trip in the moon buggy to get some rocks from a crater. If you put the pedal to the metal, it can go at 8 miles (13km) an hour! Hope that the batteries last the distance.

5 At the end of the day we can relax. The gravity is so low, you can jump higher than an Olympic athlete, even in a space suit. Luckily I packed my golf clubs. This ball should go for miles!

Rovers

Rovers are special vehicles that are designed to explore the surface of a planet or moon. Rovers take photographs and record data, which they send back to Earth. Read about some well-known robotic vehicles.

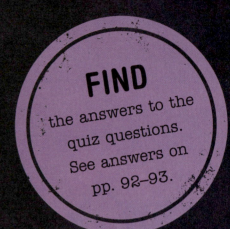

FIND the answers to the quiz questions. See answers on pp. 92–93.

Lunar Roving Vehicle
Nicknamed "moon buggy," the Lunar Roving Vehicle (LRV) was used during Apollo 15, 16, and 17 missions. It helped astronauts move around and collect a wide range of samples.

Lunokhod 1
Lunokhod 1 was one of the first Soviet vehicles to successfully explore the surface of the moon. During its 10-month mission, the rover took more than 20,000 photographs and also studied the soil on the moon.

Test Your Knowledge

Quiz

1. What was **Lunokhod 1's** mission on the moon?

2. Name the **twin rovers** that were sent to Mars.

3. What is another name for the **Lunar Roving Vehicle**?

4. Did **Perseverance** land on the moon or Mars?

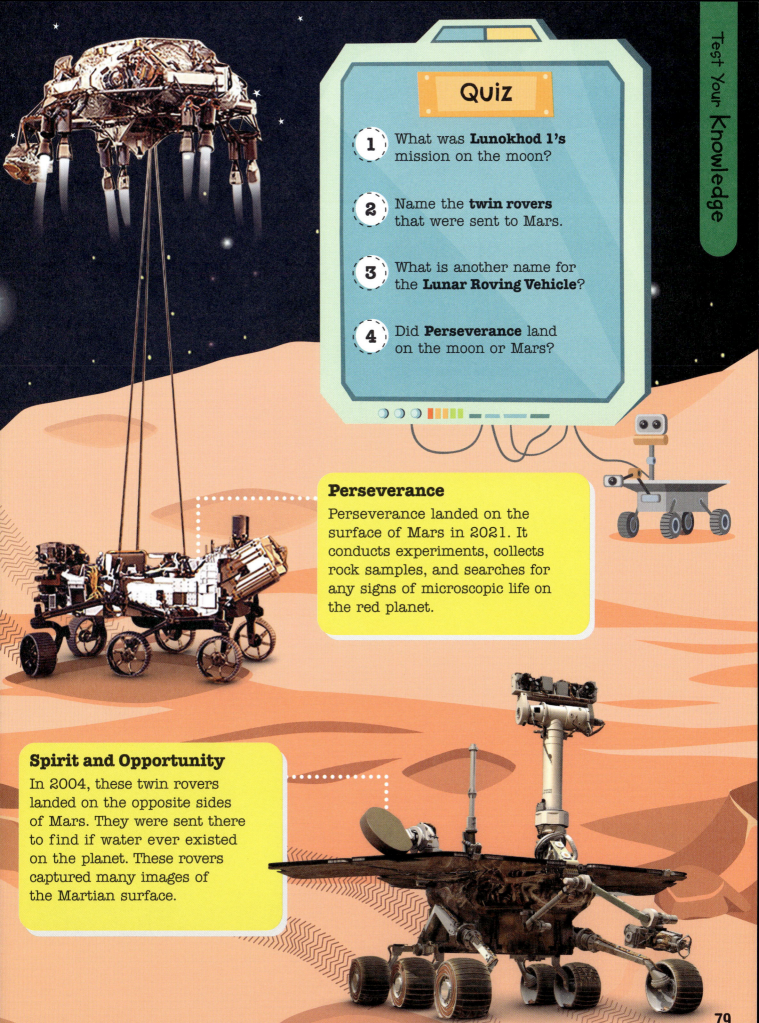

Perseverance
Perseverance landed on the surface of Mars in 2021. It conducts experiments, collects rock samples, and searches for any signs of microscopic life on the red planet.

Spirit and Opportunity
In 2004, these twin rovers landed on the opposite sides of Mars. They were sent there to find if water ever existed on the planet. These rovers captured many images of the Martian surface.

American in space
This badge marks the first US astronaut in space.

Moon landing
This mission badge celebrates man's first successful landing on the moon.

Space shuttle
The patch highlights Columbia's first orbit of Earth in 1981.

Satellite launch
This shuttle mission put an Indian satellite into space.

Mission badges

READ about these mission badges, then design your own badge.

Every time there is a space mission, members of the crew design a new badge. The badge usually shows what the astronauts are going to do on the mission, like launch a satellite. There are over 150 badges so far.

Indian visitor
India's first astronaut went to the Russian space station Salyut 7.

Floating in space
On this mission, an astronaut completed a space walk using a jet pack.

Telescope launch
Launching the Hubble telescope allowed us to see even farther into space.

Mars Pathfinder
In 1997 a robotic rover was sent to Mars to explore its surface.

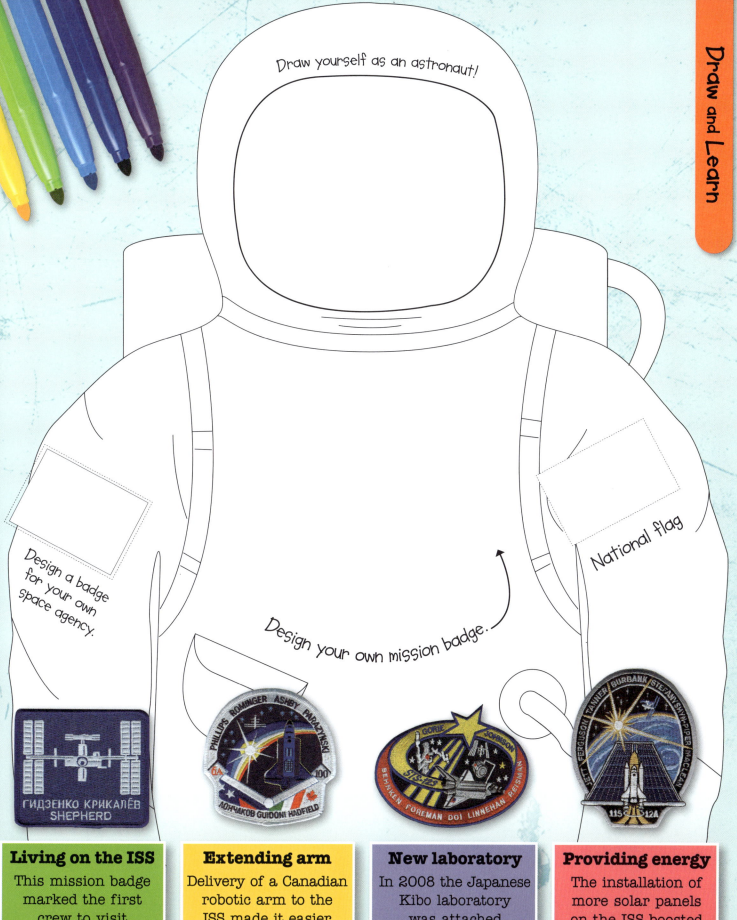

Life on Mars

COLOR this scene of a colony of astronauts living on Mars with their pet dog!

It wouldn't be easy to pack up and settle down on another planet. We would have to take everything we need—food, water, equipment, and lots of building materials—to survive for long periods.

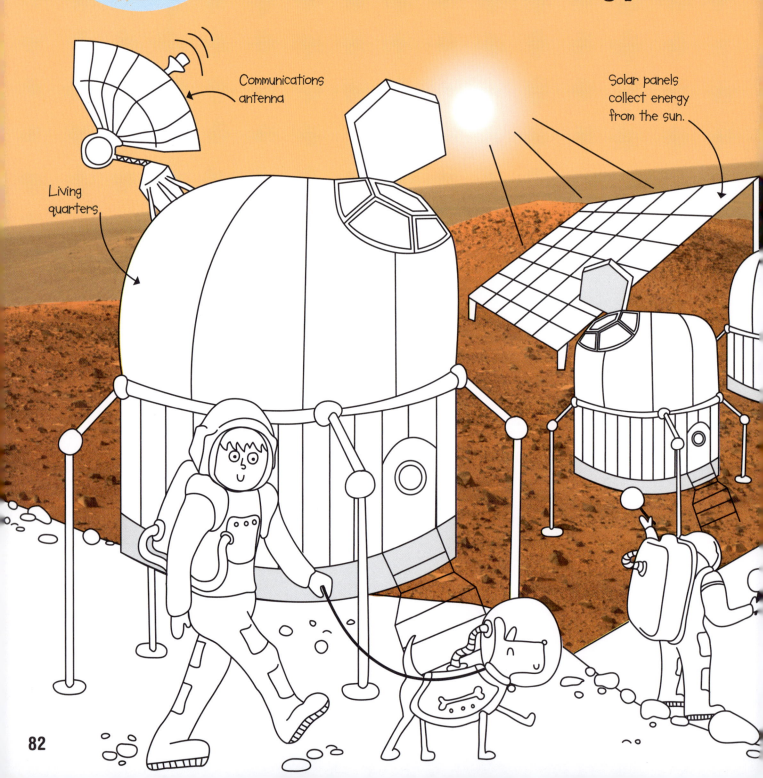

Communications antenna

Solar panels collect energy from the sun.

Living quarters

82

Destination Mars

There are plans to send people to Mars one day in the future, but with each journey taking up to 10 months, it won't be a quick trip. Conditions on Mars are harsh—it's cold, has almost no oxygen in its atmosphere, and the water is frozen. Life as a Martian would be tricky!

Facts about... Cavemen

The first Martian explorers could live in **caves** near the equator. This would **protect them** from deadly radiation and swirling dust storms that regularly sweep the surface.

Read and Create

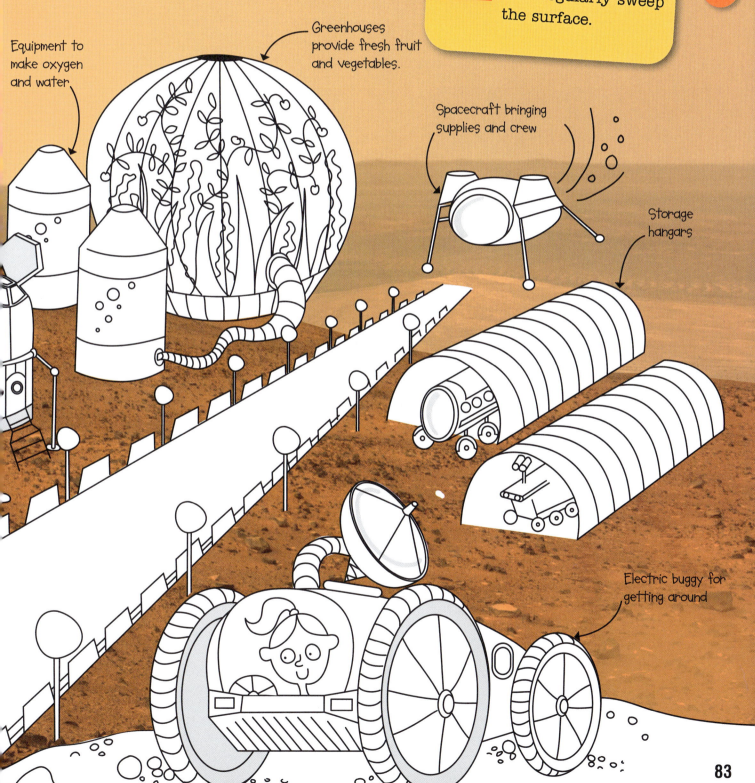

- Equipment to make oxygen and water
- Greenhouses provide fresh fruit and vegetables.
- Spacecraft bringing supplies and crew
- Storage hangars
- Electric buggy for getting around

Best-dressed astronaut

Space is not a nice place for humans. It's boiling hot in the sun and freezing cold in the shade. There's no air, but there is deadly radiation. To survive a space walk, you definitely need the right suit!

ANSWER the questions in the quiz panel. See pp. 92–93 for answers.

The helmet has two gold-plated visors that shield the astronaut from harmful solar radiation. It also contains communications and breathing equipment.

The control panel is attached to the hard upper-body section. It controls the life support systems and the communications equipment.

Life-support system

Test Your Knowledge

Facts about...

Space suits

A space suit is a complicated piece of gear. It can have as many as **16 layers** of fabric and is white to reflect sunlight. Suits are made up of different-sized pieces to match the build of the astronaut. It has to carry **enough water and oxygen** for the whole space walk.

The gloves have special grips for holding tools and are heated to keep the fingers warm.

The boots are soft and flexible so they can be slipped into footholds on the robotic arm.

Suits are made of separate parts that clamp together to make them airtight.

These colored stripes help astronauts recognize each other.

Quiz

1. What does the control panel regulate?

- a. Life-support systems
- b. Gloves
- c. Boots
- d. Helmet

2. How many layers is a space suit made of?

- a. 12
- b. 20
- c. 16
- d. 15

3. Why do the gloves have special grips?

- a. To hold tools
- b. To hold water
- c. To keep fingers warm
- d. To hold the robotic arm

Space pioneers

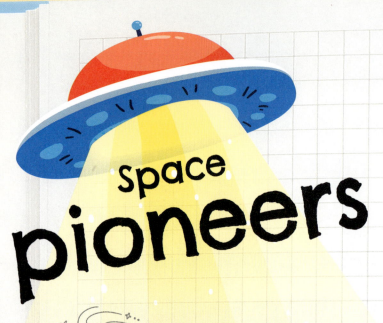

Early space explorers were the first humans to travel into space and unravel its mysteries. Let's read about some of these pioneers, who not only created history, but also paved the way for further exploration.

Yuri Gagarin

Yuri Gagarin, a Russian cosmonaut, made history when he became the first human in space on April 12, 1961. He orbited Earth in his spacecraft *Vostok 1* for 108 minutes.

TEST yourself to see how much you know about these famous space explorers!

Valentina Tereshkova

Russian cosmonaut Valentina Tereshkova was the first woman to go into space. On a solo mission in 1963, she completed 48 orbits of Earth on her three-day trip.

Neil Armstrong

On July 20, 1969, American astronaut Neil Armstrong became the first person to walk on the moon. He and his fellow astronaut Buzz Aldrin explored the lunar surface for about 2.5 hours.

Mae Jemison

A doctor, engineer, and astronaut, Mae Jemison became the first African-American woman to travel to space in 1992. During this mission, she conducted several experiments on weightlessness and motion sickness.

Peggy Whitson

Peggy Whitson, an American astronaut, set a record for the most space walks done by a woman—10. She also became the first woman commander of the ISS in 2007.

True or False

1. **Neil Armstrong** was the first human in space in 1961.

2. **Valentina Tereshkova** was the first woman to go into space in 1963.

3. **Peggy Whitson** became the first woman commander of the ISS in 2007.

Test Your Knowledge

87

space careers

A team of space experts comes together to take space exploration to newer heights and make any mission possible. If you're curious about outer space or technology, there may be a space career that could be perfect for you!

Facts about...

Virtual-reality gear
Astronauts use **virtual-reality equipment** to practice space walks. It makes them feel like they are **really in space**!

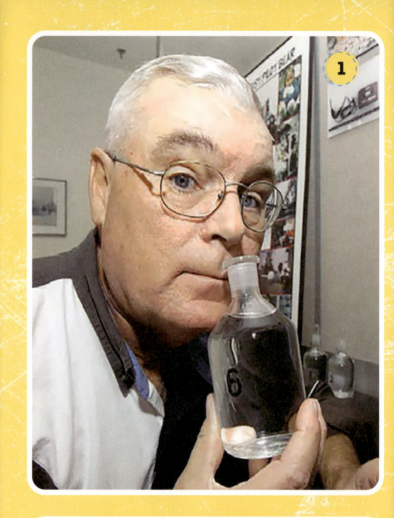

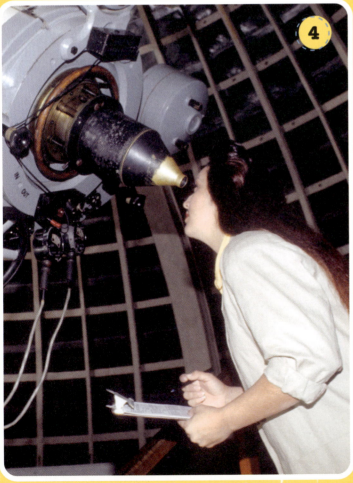

MATCH
the job descriptions to their pictures. Answers on pp. 92–93.

Match and Learn

Astronaut
An astronaut has many important things to do in space. The astronaut undergoes intense training to travel in a spacecraft, conducts experiments on space stations, and repairs space equipment.

Astronomer
An astronomer is a scientist who studies the stars, planets, galaxies, black holes, and other celestial objects. The astronomer uses telescopes to examine what these objects are and how they are formed.

Spacecraft engineer
A spacecraft engineer mostly designs and tests rovers, space stations, satellites, and probes that go into space. The engineer also develops newer technologies to help further space exploration.

Sniffer
A sniffer's main task is to smell things before sending them into space. This helps to avoid any toxic or foul smells in the spacecraft, which can be very uncomfortable for the astronauts.

All about space

Now that you've read so much about space, it's time to see how much you've learned. Take this quiz to qualify as a space geek!

1 Scientists believe there are more than **100 billion galaxies** in the universe.

2 **Auroras**, or northern lights, can be seen in the stratosphere layer of the atmosphere.

ANSWER whether each statement is true or false. Answers are on pp. 92–93.

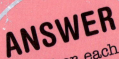

3 **Io**, one of Jupiter's moons, has **more than 80** major volcanic areas on its surface.

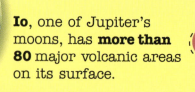

Neil Armstrong (left), Michael Collins (center), and Edwin "Buzz" Aldrin (right).

4 The *Apollo 11* crew fulfilled humanity's age-old dream of **landing on the moon**.

Test Your Knowledge

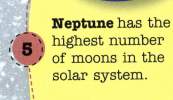

The solar panels create electricity using sunlight.

6 The **Hubble Space Telescope** was launched into space on April 24, 1993.

5 **Neptune** has the highest number of moons in the solar system.

7 A **NASA rover** that was designed to explore Mars was named **Curiosity**.

The rover has 17 cameras to take images.

8 **Space walks** conducted by astronauts usually last between **3 and 5 hours**.

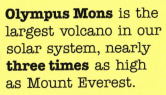

9 **Olympus Mons** is the largest volcano in our solar system, nearly **three times** as high as Mount Everest.

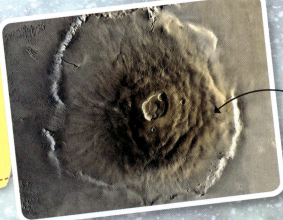

This Martian volcano is about 14 miles (22 km) high.

91

Answers

6–7
1. Page 22
2. Page 12
3. Page 18
4. Page 21
5. Page 16
6. Page 20
7. Page 8
8. Page 12
9. Page 11
10. Page 15
11. Page 17
12. Page 20

8–9
1. Skydiver
2. Meteors
3. Hot-air balloon
4. Clouds
5. Hubble Space Telescope
6. Space station

10–11
True or False?
True
1. d
2. a
3. c
4. e
5. b
6. f

14–15
True or False?
False. They do.

18–19
1. **True**   2. **True**
3. **False**. Volcanic activity keeps Earth's rocks younger than the moon's.
4. **True**   5. **True**
6. **True**

24–25
1. Page 38
2. Page 28
3. Page 35
4. Page 40
5. Page 30
6. Page 36
7. Page 31
8. Page 33
9. Page 36
10. Page 41
11. Page 38
12. Page 31

26–27
1. 88 days
2. 225 days
3. 1 year
4. 2 years
5. 12 years
6. 29.5 years
7. 84 years
8. 165 years

28–29
1. Mercury
2. Venus
3. Earth
4. Mars
5. Asteroid belt
6. Jupiter
7. Saturn
8. Uranus
9. Neptune

32–33
1. Mostly gaseous hydrogen (90%) and helium (10%)
2. 79 known moons
3. To investigate its weather and large moons
4. 10 hours

34–35
1. **True**   2. **True**
3. **False**. The rings were first seen in 1655, by Christian Huygens.
4. **True**
5. **False**. It is only twice as far from the sun as Jupiter.

36–37
1. Moon
2. Enceladus
3. Triton
4. Titan
5. Miranda
6. Ganymede

38–39
1. **True**
2. **False**. Most are pieces of comets and asteroids.
3. **True**
4. **False**. There are about 30 a year.
5. **False**. More than 70,000 have been found.
6. **True**

42–43
1. Page 50
2. Page 55
3. Page 46
4. Page 49
5. Page 44
6. Page 47
7. Page 45
8. Page 56
9. Page 58
10. Page 53
11. Page 57
12. Page 58

44–45
1. **True**   2. **True**
3. **False**. It is 275 million stars a day.
4. **True**
5. **False**. It is said to smell like raspberries!
6. **True**
7. **False**. The Soviet Union
8. **False**. 1,300 Earths

46–47
1. d
2. e
3. b
4. a
5. c

52–53
True or False?
True

56–57
1. e
2. g
3. d
4. f
5. b
6. c
7. a

60–61
1. Page 64
2. Page 67
3. Page 72
4. Page 71
5. Page 90
6. Page 80
7. Page 79
8. Page 62
9. Page 84
10. Page 74
11. Page 91
12. Page 77

68–69
True or False?
True

70–71
1. 1973
2. About 9 years
3. The Soviet Union
4. 7 years

78–79
1. To take photographs and study the lunar soil.
2. Spirit and Opportunity
3. Moon buggy
4. Mars

84–85
1. a
2. c
3. a

86–87
1. **False**. Yuri Gagarin
2. **True**   3. **True**

88–89
1. Sniffer
2. Astronaut
3. Spacecraft engineer
4. Astronomer

90–91
1. **True**
2. **False**. Thermosphere
3. **True**
4. **True**
5. **False**. Saturn
6. **False**. April 24, 1990
7. **True**
8. **False**. Between 6 and 8 hours
9. **True**

93

Glossary

asteroid
Small, rocky object that orbits between the planets

astronaut
Person who is trained to go into space

atmosphere
Layers of gases surrounding a planet, star, or moon

black hole
Region of space with such strong gravity that light cannot escape it

blue supergiant
Extremely hot and luminous star (*see luminosity*)

comet
Object made of snow, dust, and rocks orbiting the sun

constellation
Area of the sky containing a pattern of stars

cosmonaut
Astronaut from Russia

crater
Bowl-shaped hollow in an object's surface, often formed by an impact and explosion

dwarf planet
Five objects, including Pluto, are known as dwarf planets. They are smaller than the eight main planets

Earth
Our planet, the third planet from the sun

galaxy
Huge collection of stars, gas, and dust in space

gravity
Invisible force that pulls objects toward each other

illuminate
To light something up

ISS
International Space Station is a space station that orbits Earth

luminosity
Energy an object radiates into space

lunar
Belonging to the moon

mass
Amount of matter an object contains

meteor
Streak of light caused by dust entering Earth's atmosphere

meteorite
Small rock or piece of debris that falls to Earth from space

Milky Way
Spiral galaxy that contains our solar system

mission control
Place where many people work to help space missions and astronauts in space

module
Unit of a spacecraft

moon
Natural satellite of a planet

NASA
US agency responsible for space programs and research

nebula
Cloud of gas and dust in space

orbit
Path an object takes around another object, such as a planet or star

planet
Large, round object that orbits the sun, such as Mars, Venus, or Jupiter

planetary nebula
Shells of gas thrown off by a red giant star

probe
Unmanned spacecraft designed to study objects in space and send data back to Earth

protostar
Star in early stages of formation

radiation
Heat, light, or energy that is emitted out of something

red giant
Dying star that is very big and bright

red supergiant
A dying monster star

rover
Wheeled vehicle, either manned or unmanned, that is used to explore the surface of a planet or moon

satellite
Object that moves around another larger object

solar system
Sun and other objects, such as planets and moons, that orbit it

space
Mostly empty region between objects such as planets, stars, and galaxies

spacecraft
Vehicle, with or without a crew, that travels through space

space suit
Clothing worn by space travelers to provide oxygen, a radio, and protection from the environment of space

space walk
Also called Extravehicular Activity (EVA), any activity in which an astronaut goes outside a spacecraft—to make repairs or conduct an experiment

star
Huge ball of gas emitting light and heat

suborbital
A vehicle that goes into outer space at a speed not fast enough to stay in space, and comes back to Earth once its engines are shut off

sun
Star at the center of our solar system. Earth and other planets orbit the sun

supernova
Brilliant explosion, a possible stage in the death of a star

taikonaut
Astronaut from China

telescope
Instrument used to detect radiation from distant objects

universe
Everything in space, including all the stars, nebulae, planets, and galaxies

volcano
Conical mountain with a crater from which lava and gas erupts from a planetary crust

white dwarf
Dying, cooling Earth-sized star

Acknowledgments

Original edition: Design Clare Shedden, Stefan Georgiou, Charlotte Milner, Pamela Shiels; **Editorial** Wendy Horobin; **Illustration** Jake McDonald, Charlotte Milner.

DORLING KINDERSLEY would like to thank: Rea Pikula for proofreading; Marie Greenwood, Kathleen Teece, Niharika Prabhakar, Kritika Gupta, and Manisha Majithia for editorial support.

The publisher would like to thank the following for their kind permission to reproduce their photographs:

(Key: a-above; b-below/bottom; c-center; f-far; l-left; r-right; t-top)

4 Dorling Kindersley: Dave King / Rotring UK Ltd (fcl). **5 Dorling Kindersley:** Dan Crisp (tr); D. Hurst (fcr). **Shutterstock.com:** (br). **6 Dreamstime.com:** Lunamarina (tr). **ESA:** ESA / DLR / FU-Berlin-G. Neukum (cl). **NASA:** ESA, and the Hubble Heritage Team (STScI / AURA)-ESA / Hubble Collaboration / B. Whitmore (Space Telescope Science Institute) (br). **7 Dreamstime.com:** Jfunk (cr). **NASA:** JPL (tr); JPL Caltech / P.Appleton et al. (br) (cl). **8 Dorling Kindersley:** Fotolia: Pekka Jaakkola / Luminis (br). **Dreamstime.com:** Rhonda Kuzba (c). **9 Dorling Kindersley:** Dan Crisp (cl, c). **11 NASA:** (t) (b). **12 Science Photo Library:** DETLEV VAN RAVENSWAAY (ca). **Dreamstime.com:** Lunamarina (bl); Showvector (cl). **NASA:** JPL (tr); USGS (clb). **13 Science Photo Library:** MARK GARLICK (tl). **NASA:** R. Ellis (Caltech), and the HUDF 2012 Team (tr). **14 Dreamstime.com:** Valeriy Novikov / Ru3apr (tl). **NASA:** (cla). **14-15 NASA:** (c). **15 Dorling Kindersley:** Fotolia: Pekka Jaakkola / Luminis (cr). **Dreamstime.com:** Jfunk (cra). **NASA:** ESA / Alex Lutkus (crb). **16-17 Dreamstime.com:** Alinamd (c). **20 ESA:** ESA (c). **ESO:** ALMA (ESO / NAOJ / NRAO); ESO / Y. Beletsky (cb); ESO / J. Emerson / VISTA (cr). **NASA:** E / PO, Sonoma State University, Aurore Simonnet (ca); ESA Hubble (tc); JPL (tr). **21 ESO:** ESO / Y. Beletsky (clb). **NASA:** ESA / Alex Lutkus (crb); DOE / Fermi LAT Collaboration, Capella Observatory, and Ilana Feain, Tim Cornwell, and Ron Ekers (CSIRO / ATNF), R. Morganti (ASTRON), and N. Junkes (MPIfR) (tl); JPL-Caltech (cra) (c); JPL-Caltech (cla); CXC & J.Vaughan (ca). **22 ESA:** ESA / DLR / FU-Berlin-G.Neukum (tl). **NASA:** JHUAPL / SwRI (cra); Johns Hopkins University Applied Physics Laboratory / Southwest Research Institute (ca); JPL-Caltech (c); JPL-Caltech (cb) (clb) (fclb). **ESA:** ESA / DLR / FU-Berlin (G. Neukum) (t); ESA / DLR / FU-Berlin-G.Neukum (b). **24 Dreamstime.com:** Eraxion (cla). **NASA:** JPL / University of Arizona (cr); JPL-Caltech (bl). **25 Dorling Kindersley:** Colin Keates / Natural History Museum, London (cr). **Dreamstime.com:** Showvector (tr). **NASA:** JPL-Caltech / Cornell / USGS (tl); JPL-Caltech / Cornell / ASU (br). **30 NASA:** JPL-Caltech / Univ. of Arizona (c); JPL-Caltech (bl); JPL / University of Arizona (bc). **30-31 NASA:** JPL-Caltech / Cornell Univ. / Arizona State Univ. (c). **31 NASA:** JPL-Caltech / Cornell / ASU (tl); JPL / MSSS (crb); JPL-Caltech / MSSS / Texas A&M Univ. (bc); JPL / Arizona State University (cla); JPL-Caltech / Cornell / USGS (clb). **33 Dorling Kindersley:** NASA (tl). **Dreamstime.com:** Showvector (t, br). **ESA:** NASA, ESA and M. Wong and I. de Pater (University of California, Berkeley) (crb). **NASA:** JPL / DLR (c); JPL / University of Arizona (ca/Io); JPL / DLR (c). **35 Dreamstime.com:** Showvector (tc). **36-37 Dreamstime.com:** Showvector. **37 Dorling Kindersley: Getty Images:** Stocktrek RF (cb); NASA / JPL (c). **NASA:** JPL / University of Arizona (ca); JPL cb/Triton). **38 Dorling Kindersley:** Colin Keates / Natural History Museum, London (clb). **Dreamstime.com:** Eraxion (bc). **ESO:** ESO / C. Malin (ca). **40 ESA:** NASA, ESA and M. Wong and I. de Pater (University of California, Berkeley) (tl). **NASA:** Johns Hopkins University Applied Physics Laboratory / Southwest Research Institute (bl); JPL-Caltech / Space Science Institute (cl); Johns Hopkins University Applied Physics Laboratory / Southwest Research Institute (fbl/pluto); JPL / University of Arizona (fbl); JPL / University of Arizona (ca); JPL / University of Arizona (fcrb); JPL / DLR (crb). **42 Depositphotos Inc:** brgfx (bl). **ESO:** ESO / Y. Beletsky (br). **NASA:** ESA and AURA / Caltech (cr); JPL-Caltech / ESA / Harvard-Smithsonian CfA (cl) (cra). **Shutterstock.com:** Ryzhkov Sergey (tl). **43 ESO:** ESO (bl). **NASA:** ESA, H. Teplitz and M. Rafelski (IPAC / Caltech), A. Koekemoer (STScI), R. Windhorst (Arizona State University), and Z. Levay (STScI) (tl); ESA (cla); ESA and the Hubble SM4 ERO Team (c); ESA / Hubble and the Hubble Heritage Tea (cr); ESA, Andrew Fruchter (STScI), and the ERO team (STScI + ST-ECF) (tr). **44-45 Dreamstime.com:** Roman Egorov (*12). **45 NASA:** ESA, H. Teplitz and M. Rafelski (IPAC / Caltech), A. Koekemoer (STScI), R. Windhorst (Arizona State University), and Z. Levay (STScI) (tl); ESA (tr). **46 NASA:** ESA, and E. Peng (Peking University, Beijing) (bl); JPL-Caltech / ESA / Harvard-Smithsonian CfA (cl). **47 ESA:** NASA, ESA and the Hubble Heritage Team (STScI / AURA). Acknowledgment: J. Gallagher (University of Wisconsin), M. Mountain (STScI) and P. Puxley (NSF) (c). **NASA:** ESA, and The Hubble Heritage Team (STScI / AURA) (tc); ESA, Y. Izotov (Main Astronomical Observatory, Kyiv, UA) and T. Thuan (University of Virginia) (br). **48 NASA:** ESA / Hubble & NASA (tr); ESA, and P. Challis and R. Kirshner (cb); H. Bond (STScI), R. Ciardullo (PSU), WFPC2, HST, NASA (crb) (cl). **48-49 R. Jay GaBany:** © 2004-2022 by R Jay GaBany, Cosmotography.com. **49 Dreamstime.com:** Monkographic (bl). **ESO:** ESO / Digitized Sky Survey 2. Acknowledgment: Davide De Martin. (tc). **NASA:** ESA and AURA / Caltech (cl); X-ray Image CXC / ASU / J. Hester et al.; (cr). **50 Shutterstock.com:** Ryzhkov Sergey (c). **51 Akira Fujii/David Malin Images:** © Akira Fujii / David Malin Images (tr). **52 NASA:** CXC / M.Weiss; CXC / M.Weiss (tr); CXC / M.Weiss (cra). **53 ESA:** ESA / Hubble and Digitized Sky Survey 2. (br); NASA / ESA, The Hubble Heritage Team STScI / AURA (bc). **NASA:** ESA and G. Bacon (STScI) (tr) (cla); X-ray: CXC / University of Amsterdam / N.Rea et al; Optical: DSS (crb). **54 Alamy Stock Photo:** Alamy: D. Hurst (clb). **NASA:** ESA (ca); JPL-Caltech / R. Hurt (IPAC) (c). **55 Alain Riazuelo:** A. Riazuelo / IAP / SU / CNRS (c). **ESA:** ESA / Hubble, L. Calçada (ESO) (ca). **NASA:** CXC / SAO (bl); ESA, and The Hubble Heritage Team (STScI / AURA) (tl) (tr). **56 ESA:** NASA, ESA, M. Robberto (Space Telescope Science Institute / ESA) and the Hubble Space Telescope Orion Treasury Project Team (tl). **NASA:** CXC / JPL-Caltech / STScI (cla); ESA, Andrew Fruchter (STScI), and the ERO team (STScI + ST-ECF) (cr). **57 ESO:** ESO (cr). **NASA:** ESA and the Hubble SM4 ERO Team (tl); ESA, HEIC, and The Hubble Heritage Team (STScI / AURA) (bl); ESA, Mario Livio (STScI), Hubble 20th Anniversary Team (STScI) (cra). **60 Alamy Stock Photo:** NG Images / Alamy Stock Photo (cl); NG Images / Alamy Stock Photo (b). **Dreamstime.com:** Dimazzzel (cr) (crb). **NASA:** (br). **Shutterstock.com:** (tr). **61 Dreamstime.com:** Dannyphoto80 (tl); Yauhen Paleski (cr); Pavlo Plakhotia (cla). **ESA:** ESA - A. Gerst (bl). **Getty Images:** Hulton Deutsch / Contributor (crb). **NASA:** USGS (bc). **63 Dreamstime.com:** Ratselmeister (c). **64 Alamy Stock Photo:** Adrian Mann / Stocktrek Images (br). **Dreamstime.com:** Nerthuz (cb). **ESA:** ESA-Pierre Carril, 2014 (cl); ESA-D. Ducros, 2014 (bc). **NASA:** (tl) (cl) (fcr); Kim Shiflett (bl). **64-65 Alamy Stock Photo:** NG Images / Alamy Stock Photo. **65 Dorling Kindersley:** Dave King / Rotring UK Ltd (br). **66-67 Dreamstime.com:** Andreykuzmin (window background). **66 Depositphotos Inc:** denisik11 (window). **Shutterstock.com:** (b). **67 Depositphotos Inc:** denisik11 (window). **68 NASA:** (cla). **69 NASA:** (tr) (bc) (cr) (c). **70-71 Dreamstime.com:** Karenr (graphx4). **NASA:** Ames Research Center / Daniel Rutter. **70 NASA:** (cr). **Science Photo Library:** DETLEV VAN RAVENSWAAY / SCIENCE PHOTO LIBRARY (bl). **71 NASA:** (tr). **72-73 NASA:** ISS > Digital Camera. **74 Dorling Kindersley:** Jerry Young (br). **75 Dreamstime.com:** Isselee (bl). **Getty Images:** Sovfoto / Contributor (tl). **NASA:** (cr). **76-77 Dorling Kindersley:** Dorling Kindersley: NASA (b). **79 NASA:** JPL-Caltech (tl); JPL-Caltech (br). **80 NASA:** (tl) (tc) (tr) (bl) (bc) (br). **81 NASA:** (bl) (bc) (br) (fbr). **82-83 NASA:** JPL-Caltech / Cornell Univ. / Arizona State Univ. **84-85 ESA:** ESA - A. Gerst. **86 Alamy Stock Photo:** Archive Collection / Alamy Stock Photo (cl). **Getty Images:** Heritage Images / Contributor (br). **86-87 Dreamstime.com:** Karenr (c). **87 NASA:** (tr) (cla) (br). **88 NASA:** (tr) (br). **88-89 Dreamstime.com:** Yufa12379 (c). **89 Alamy Stock Photo:** Ted Foxx / Alamy Stock Photo (bl). **NASA:** (tl). **90-91 NASA:** Mehmet Hakan zsaraç (c). **90 Alamy Stock Photo:** NG Images / Alamy Stock Photo (cl). **Dreamstime.com:** Markus Schieder (tr). **NASA:** (bl). **91 Alamy Stock Photo:** Maria Temereva / Alamy Stock Vector (tl). **NASA:** ESA (tr); JPL-Caltech (clb) (cr); USGS (bc). **92 NASA:** ESA / Alex Lutkus (br). **93 NASA:** ESA, Mario Livio (STScI), Hubble 20th Anniversary Team (STScI) (br). **94 Dreamstime.com:** Roman Egorov (cr, tr). **95 Dreamstime.com:** Isselee (tc/rabbit); Monkographic (br); Yauhen Paleski (tc). **96 Dreamstime.com:** Dannyphoto80 (cb); Pavlo Plakhotia (br).

Cover images: *Front:* **Alamy Stock Photo:** D. Hurst cb; **Dorling Kindersley:** NASA cra; **Dreamstime.com:** Clearviewstock c.

All other images © Dorling Kindersley.